Toni Eatts

illustrations by Jo Palme

Angus&Robertson
An imprint of HarperCollins*Publishers*

*In loving memory of
my mother, Joan Eatts,
who shared with me her delight in books.*

How to Use This Book

Your intuition already knows the answers to any questions you may have about your relationships. However it is often difficult to interpret your intuition and recognise what is happening in your life. That is where this book will help.

Loves Me Loves Me Not is filled with quotes that cover all aspects of love — the passion and the pain. Hold a clear question in your mind that can only have a 'Yes' or 'No' answer. For example, 'Will _ _ _ call me?' or 'Is _ _ _ serious about me?'

Open the book and read the quote. It is your intuition's reply to your question. Think of your intuition as a wise, old Chinese sage. Rather than tell you exactly what to do it is more likely to give you something to think about and work out for yourself.

Sometimes you will draw a direct reply that is easy to interpret. At other times the reply may be more subtle. If this happens take note of the quote and keep an open mind. Often your intuition can be a step ahead of you and the meaning of the quote will become apparent in a day or so.

You can also use this book to:

- Clarify your feelings about a relationship by asking, 'How do I really feel about _ _ _ ?'

- Do some 'psychic spying' and find out how your partner feels about you by asking, 'How does _ _ _ feel about me?' or 'What does this relationship really mean to _ _ _ ?'

- Heal rifts in your relationship. If you've had a tiff ask the book for the right words to say or send to your loved one.

- Help you express your feelings for everyone you love, from your family and friends, to your work colleagues or even your boss! Hold a mental picture of that person, ask for the appropriate words and open the book.

- Have fun. Bring the book out at dinner parties, hand it around the table and get everyone to reveal their question and the answer they receive. The revelations will spark lively conversation.

A word of caution — you should remain as objective as possible. Always check the message the book gives you with the events in your life. If you ask whether your new partner will marry you and you receive a 'No' answer, don't end the relationship without checking with the person first. Likewise, be wary of ignoring negative responses that might be timely warnings. Take a closer look at your partner, their behaviour and your feelings and then make a decision.

Here's hoping *Loves Me Loves Me Not* enriches your experience of love — its presence, its healing and especially its magic.

LOVES ME ~ LOVES ME NOT

How say you? Let us, O my dove,

Let us be unashamed of soul,

As earth lies bare to heaven above!

How is it under our control

To love or not to love?

ROBERT BROWNING

LOVES ME ~ LOVES ME NOT

LOVES ME ~ LOVES ME NOT

Although I may love you,
I do not own you.
You are simply part of my story
as I am part of yours.

DR ROSIE KING

*If you want to know
how much you love yourself,
see how much you're loved.*

LOVES ME ~ LOVES ME NOT

LOVES ME ~ LOVES ME NOT

LOVES ME ~ LOVES ME NOT

*Come live with me and be my love,
And we will all the pleasures prove.*

CHRISTOPHER MARLOWE

Friendship is a priceless treasure that outlives numerous love affairs.

LOVES ME ~ LOVES ME NOT

LOVES ME ~ LOVES ME NOT

Forgiveness is the tool to dig down through the layers of anger, pain, hurt and guilt to real love.

BARBARA AND TERRY TEBO

When I'm with you

I feel myself unfold

like a flower.

LOVES ME ~ LOVES ME NOT

LOVES ME ~ LOVES ME NOT

If thou must love me, let it be for naught Except for love's sake only.

ELIZABETH BARRETT BROWNING

You think
I left first.
But really
it was you.

LOVES ME ~ LOVES ME NOT

LOVES ME ~ LOVES ME NOT

LOVES ME ~ LOVES ME NOT

I want to give you more of my love.

All your kisses and fine words are not enough to heal my pain.

LOVES ME ~ LOVES ME NOT

LOVES ME ~ LOVES ME NOT

LOVES ME ~ LOVES ME NOT

Merged in a moment which gives me at last

You around me for once, you beneath me,

above me ~

Me, sure that, despite of time future, time past,

This tick of life~time's one moment you

love me!

ROBERT BROWNING

LOVES ME ~ LOVES ME NOT

*The only person
you have the power
to change
is yourself.*

LOVES ME ~ LOVES ME NOT

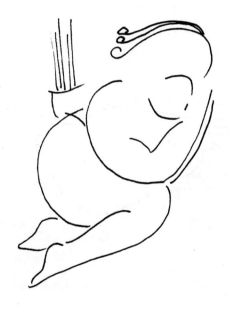

LOVES ME ~ LOVES ME NOT

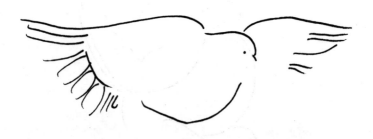

A successful relationship calls for commitment, love and chemistry.

TOBY GREEN

LOVES ME ~ LOVES ME NOT

Did I ever promise

that I would be true to you?

LOVES ME ~ LOVES ME NOT

LOVES ME ~ LOVES ME NOT

Intimacy is when I invite you to tell me exactly who you are on the inside and you do the same.

TOBY GREEN

LOVES ME ~ LOVES ME NOT

How do I love thee? Let me count the ways.

. . . I love thee with the breath,

Smiles, tears, of all my life! ~ and, if God choose,

I shall but love thee better after death.

ELIZABETH BARRETT BROWNING

LOVES ME ~ LOVES ME NOT

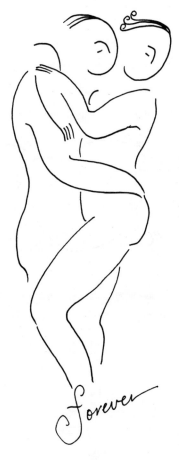

LOVES ME ~ LOVES ME NOT

*Don't listen
to your friends.
Love me anyway.*

Indeed I must confess,
When souls mix 'tis an happiness,
But not complete till bodies too do join,
And both our wholes into one whole combine.

ABRAHAM COWLEY

LOVES ME ~ LOVES ME NOT

LOVES ME ~ LOVES ME NOT

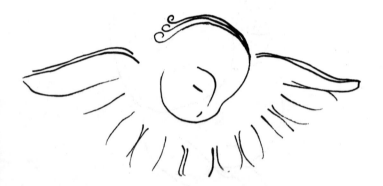

Lust is nature's way of convincing you you're in love.

*Trust in a relationship is like
a sandcastle on a beach,
gradually built a spadeful at a time,
subject to the waves and winds of life.
Creating trust is hard work.
Let us cooperate and build
a mighty fortress of trust together.*

DR ROSIE KING

LOVES ME ~ LOVES ME NOT

LOVES ME ~ LOVES ME NOT

LOVES ME ~ LOVES ME NOT

Be honest.
You saw the danger signs
stamped all over me
and ignored them anyway.

*W*hen I hurt

I hide.

LOVES ME ~ LOVES ME NOT

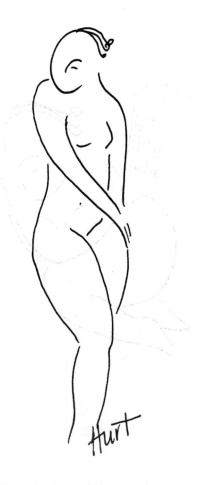

LOVES ME ~ LOVES ME NOT

*You are my angel.
Carry me on your
wings of desire.*

LOVES ME ~ LOVES ME NOT

Rejecting me you reject love.

This is why you are always looking for love

But never find it.

FROM 'THE GREAT SPIRIT SPEAKS'
AUTHOR UNKNOWN

LOVES ME ~ LOVES ME NOT

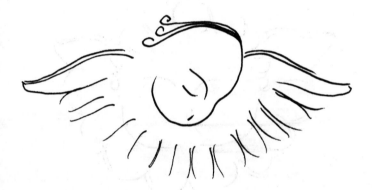

LOVES ME ~ LOVES ME NOT

*B*e true

to yourself.

LOVES ME ~ LOVES ME NOT

*M*an's love is of man's life a thing apart,
'Tis woman's whole existance.

GEORGE GORDON BYRON

LOVES ME ~ LOVES ME NOT

LOVES ME ~ LOVES ME NOT

LOVES ME ~ LOVES ME NOT

*I need to feel safe
before I can
love you.*

LOVES ME ~ LOVES ME NOT

Wild Nights ~ Wild Nights!
Were I with thee
Wild Nights should be
Our luxury!

EMILY DICKINSON

LOVES ME ~ LOVES ME NOT

LOVES ME ~ LOVES ME NOT

*Our love was like thistledown.
We blew it away.*

Commitment is the grown~up way to say 'I love you'.

DR ROSIE KING

LOVES ME ~ LOVES ME NOT

LOVES ME ~ LOVES ME NOT

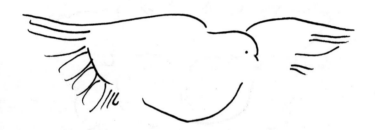

Right feelings

right person

wrong time.

LOVES ME ~ LOVES ME NOT

And that my delight may be solidly fixed,
Let the friend and the lover be handsomely mixed,
In whose tender bosom my soul might confide,
Whose kindness can sooth me, whose counsel could guide.

LADY MARY WORTLEY MONTAGU

LOVES ME ~ LOVES ME NOT

LOVES ME ~ LOVES ME NOT

*Play with me.
I just want
to have fun.*

*T*ime heals
all pain.

LOVES ME ~ LOVES ME NOT

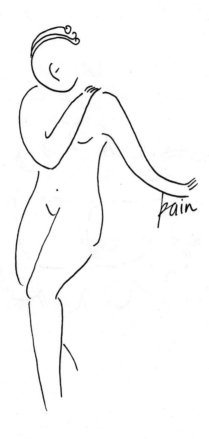

LOVES ME ~ LOVES ME NOT

LOVES ME ~ LOVES ME NOT

Hither my love!

Here I am! here!

With this just~sustain'd note I announce myself to you,

This gentle call is for you my love, for you.

WALT WHITMAN

I'm trying to tell you what I feel inside.

LOVES ME ~ LOVES ME NOT

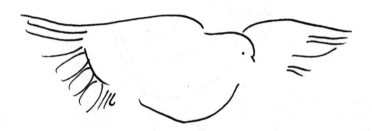

LOVES ME ~ LOVES ME NOT

LOVES ME ~ LOVES ME NOT

Being in a loving relationship doesn't mean you have to give up your freedom.

*In all phases of love
two helpful remedies
are prayer and humour.*

DR LLOYD WAGNER

LOVES ME ~ LOVES ME NOT

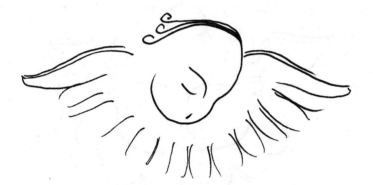

LOVES ME ~ LOVES ME NOT

LOVES ME ~ LOVES ME NOT

My love involves the love before;

My love is vaster passion now;

Though mixed with God and Nature thou,

I seem to love thee more and more.

LORD TENNYSON

It is possible to love more than one person at the same time.

LOVES ME ~ LOVES ME NOT

LOVES ME ~ LOVES ME NOT

LOVES ME ~ LOVES ME NOT

Doubt thou the stars are fire;

Doubt that the sun doth move;

Doubt truth to be a liar;

But never doubt I love.

WILLIAM SHAKESPEARE

LOVES ME ~ LOVES ME NOT

*Be a resident

in your love life,

not a tourist.*

DR LLOYD WAGNER

LOVES ME ~ LOVES ME NOT

LOVES ME ~ LOVES ME NOT

LOVES ME ~ LOVES ME NOT

Who is more frightened?
You or I?

LOVES ME ~ LOVES ME NOT

For a love that will never change
A love that will never die
A love that is ever new.
Turn to me
Acknowledge me
Accept me
And you will know such love
Here and now.
Together we will restore the world
To order and to beauty.

FROM 'THE GREAT SPIRIT SPEAKS'
AUTHOR UNKNOWN

LOVES ME ~ LOVES ME NOT

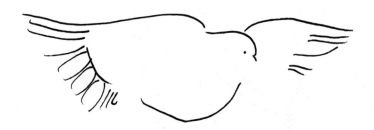

LOVES ME ~ LOVES ME NOT

Love is life's end; an end but never ending;

All joys, all sweets, all happiness awarding;

Love is life's reward, rewarded in rewarding.

EDMUND SPENCER

You long for the adult me,
but refuse to honour my inner child.

LOVES ME ~ LOVES ME NOT

LOVES ME ~ LOVES ME NOT

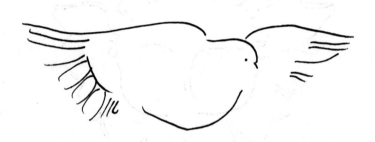

LOVES ME ~ LOVES ME NOT

I dreamed that I stood in a valley, and amid sighs,
For happy lovers passed two by two where I stood;
And I dreamed my lost love came stealthily out of the wood.

W. B. YEATS

I don't teach you,

I love you.

The love will teach you.

GREG MEYER

LOVES ME ~ LOVES ME NOT

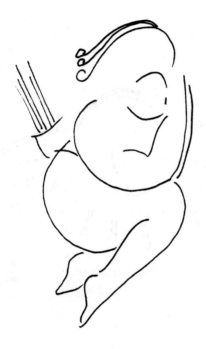

LOVES ME ~ LOVES ME NOT

There is no such thing as 'the one'. When you're ready to have a relationship, the person sitting next to you on the bus will be 'the one'.

TOBY GREEN

LOVES ME ~ LOVES ME NOT

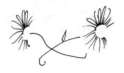

Ring out your bells, let mourning shows be spread,
For Love is dead.

SIR PHILIP SIDNEY

LOVES ME ~ LOVES ME NOT

LOVES ME ~ LOVES ME NOT

LOVES ME ~ LOVES ME NOT

*The object of dating is not to see if you can become exactly what the other person wants.
It's to see how the other person reacts to you being yourself.*

RUDY GUERRA

LOVES ME ~ LOVES ME NOT

Love is like a souffle ~
it collapses under
the weight of expectation.

LOVES ME ~ LOVES ME NOT

LOVES ME ~ LOVES ME NOT

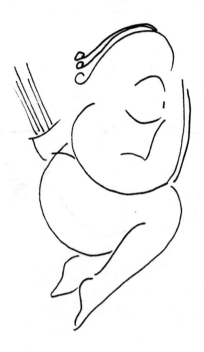

LOVES ME ~ LOVES ME NOT

Just when I seemed about to learn!
Where is the thread now? Off again!
The old trick! Only I discern ~
Infinite passion, and the pain
Of finite hearts that yearn.

ROBERT BROWNING

*True love
is never in a hurry.*

DR LLOYD WAGNER

LOVES ME ~ LOVES ME NOT

LOVES ME ~ LOVES ME NOT

*Love is forgiving
and love is for giving.*

GREG MEYER

LOVES ME ~ LOVES ME NOT

Remember me when I am gone away,

. . . Yet if you should forget me for a while

And afterwards remember, do not grieve:

. . . Better by far you should forget and smile

Than that you should remember and be sad.

CHRISTINA ROSSETTI

LOVES ME ~ LOVES ME NOT

LOVES ME ~ LOVES ME NOT

LOVES ME ~ LOVES ME NOT

I only deserve the best.

Love seeks no cause beyond itself and no fruit;

It is its own fruit, its own enjoyment.

I love because I love;

I love in order that I may love.

ST BERNARD OF CLAIRVAUX

LOVES ME ~ LOVES ME NOT

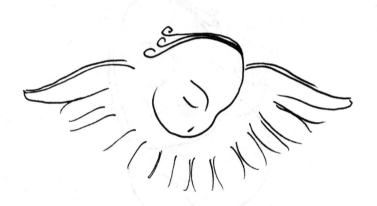

LOVES ME ~ LOVES ME NOT

Please call me.
I'm too proud
to call you.

LOVES ME ~ LOVES ME NOT

*W*ater, water I desire,
*H*ere's a house of flesh on fire.

ROBERT HERRICK

LOVES ME ~ LOVES ME NOT

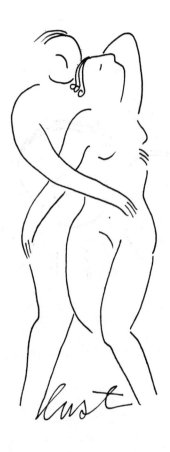

LOVES ME ~ LOVES ME NOT

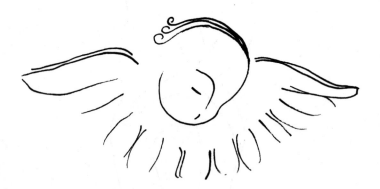

LOVES ME ~ LOVES ME NOT

When there is unconditional love there is no judgement.

BARBARA AND TERRY TEBO

LOVES ME ~ LOVES ME NOT

Believe me, if all these endearing young charms,
Which I gaze on so fondly today,
Were to change by tomorrow, and fleet in my arms,
Like fairy~gifts fading away,
Thou wouldst still be adored, as this moment thou art.

THOMAS MOORE

LOVES ME ~ LOVES ME NOT

LOVES ME ~ LOVES ME NOT

Courtship is when you're on your best behaviour. It never gets any better than this.

RUDY GUERRA

LOVES ME ~ LOVES ME NOT

The truth allows healing.
Love does the healing.

GREG MEYER

LOVES ME ~ LOVES ME NOT

LOVES ME ~ LOVES ME NOT

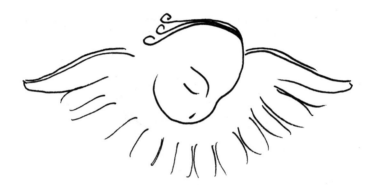

LOVES ME ~ LOVES ME NOT

*What prevents you
from getting
the love you want?*

LOVES ME ~ LOVES ME NOT

How much I love I know not, life not known,

Save as one unit I would add love by;

But this I know, my being is but thine own ~

Fused from its separateness by ecstasy.

THOMAS HARDY

LOVES ME ~ LOVES ME NOT

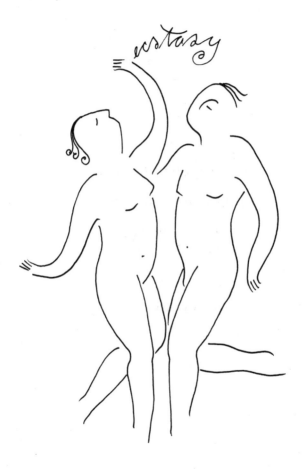

Ultimately there are only two choices ~ To Risk or To Rot.

GREG MEYER

LOVES ME ~ LOVES ME NOT

LOVES ME ~ LOVES ME NOT

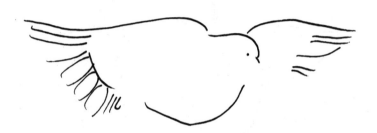

LOVES ME ~ LOVES ME NOT

Where there is no love, put love in, and you will draw love out.

ST JOHN OF THE CROSS

LOVES ME ~ LOVES ME NOT

Love teaches

more than logic.

GREG MEYER

Acknowledgments

Many people have inspired me with their wisdom and given me insights into the wonders of love. They know who they are and I thank them. I also thank the following people for generously allowing their quotes to appear in this book:

- ~ Toby Green, relationships psychologist
- ~ Rudy Guerra, counsellor
- ~ Dr Rosie King, sex therapist, columnist for *Woman's Day* and regular on radio and television
- ~ Greg Meyer, educational consultant and corporate trainer
- ~ Transworld Publishing, for quotations from Barbara and Terry Tebo's *Free to Be Me* (Doubleday, 1993)
- ~ Dr Lloyd Wagner, psychologist, specialising in male studies

An Angus & Robertson Publication

Angus&Robertson, an imprint of
HarperCollins*Publishers*
25 Ryde Road, Pymble, Sydney, NSW 2073, Australia
31 View Road, Glenfield, Auckland 10, New Zealand

First published in Australia in 1994

Copyright © Toni Eatts 1994

This book is copyright.
Apart from any fair dealing for the purposes of private study,
research, criticism or review, as permitted under the Copyright Act,
no part may be reproduced by any process without written
permission. Inquiries should be addressed to the publishers.

National Library of Australia
Cataloguing-in-Publication data:

Eatts, Toni.
Loves me loves me not.
ISBN 0 207 18253 1.

1. Love - Quotations, maxims, etc. I. Title.

152.41

Printed in Hong Kong

9 8 7 6 5 4 3 2 1
94 95 96 97